Copyright

Disclaimer:

All advice in the book is advice and not a guarantee. The strategies in this book are designed to help give you the best chances at finding a job. However the author makes no guarantees that you will be successful in your search.

Welcome to a very exciting time in your career.

CHAPTER 1 Dream Jobs Don't Happen By Accident

There are no short cuts to success. There are ways to accelerate you on your journey. One of the best ways to grow faster is to learn from people further down the path you wish to take. This book is a collection of tactics and strategies that have been compiled to give you a leg up on your competition. If you recently graduated or will be graduating soon from a college or university level computer science program, this book is for you. Congratulations on your achievements thus far. Getting through the college software engineering course load is an achievement worth celebrating. You are not done yet. The real work is just beginning. That work starts with finding your first professional position after college.

Breaking into the software development industry can be hard with out experience. You are about to learn a strategy and many tactics for standing out from the crowd so that you can target great positions and land a great first software job.

Getting A Job Is A Full Time Job

Getting a job doesn't happen on its own. It is a non-linear process that will take time and effort. You may not see results right away. Rest assured that if you follow the tactics and strategies in this book and invest time and effort every day you will set yourself up for the best opportunities out there and increase your chance of finding that first development job.

Your job search is like the last mile in a marathon, getting your degree took many years of study and effort. I've seen too many fresh graduates fail to make the leap into the real development jobs they've been training for because the job search proved too daunting. Don't let this last obstacle get in your way to the career you've been working towards. This journey will take discipline and investment but the pay off is worth it.

You need to dedicate at least 20 to 40 hours a week of solid effort during your job search. I recommend making your job this job search until you find your first professional position. This isn't something you can do in one day and then just wait for a job to land in your lap. Getting your first job can be difficult. Spending 40 hours a week on your search and improving yourself will pay dividends. You will need to spend time becoming the candidate employers are looking for and that will take time and effort. This isn't as simple as filling out resumes or posting on a few job boards. There are many little tasks you need to do consistently to be successful. You will need to build and work your network. Follow up on conversations, send thank you notes. You will be busy tailoring your resumé for each opportunity and doing a lot of real work. Finding a job is a full-time job. When you treat it like a full-time job that puts you at a major advantage compared to your competition. You have a degree, but you are not entitled to any job. Each employer you interact with is searching for and will pick the candidates they believe are the best candidates they can find. Nobody has to offer you a job. You have to sell your skills and abilities and entice employers to offer you a job. This first job search will be the hardest job search of your career.

Set yourself up for success by committing fully to the process. Set up healthy habits, like waking up at a reasonable time every day. Dedicate at least 4 to 8 solid hours every weekday on job prep and job search related activities. Get a notebook and use it to track your tasks completed, follow-ups to be made and relationships established. Be sure to take care of your body, and stay well groomed, because you are going to be judged by first impressions. Taking your search seriously is one of the best career investments you can make if you do this well you will set yourself up for success for many years to come.

Step By Step Action Guide Chapter 1

Follow these quick action steps at the end of each chapter to set yourself up for a better chance of job search success.

•Go get a professional hair cut

•Go out and buy an interviewing outfit. (This can wait till you schedule your first interview, but if you shop online you may want to order it early)

•Buy a bulk box of 100 thank you cards and stamps and commit to using them. You will probably find a job well before you use them all. But they are good to use after you have a job too.

•Get a notebook and make it your job search notebook.

•Commit to your job search like it's a full-time job.

The Employment Market

It's important to realize that you will be participating in a market. You are selling your skills and time for money and a benefits package. You are looking for a company that needs to use your skills and time to accomplish their mission so that they can make more money for their owners or shareholders. It's also important to understand that as a software engineer you will be working on the very circuitry that will be running the company, its brains. Software is one of the strongest levers businesses and organizations have to automate tasks and serve customers predictably, efficiently and at scale. And that's why the world needs lots of great software developers.

A great developer is many times more productive than an average developer. This unique attribute of the developer landscape creates a logical business case for paying better than the competition even if that means paying more for each team member than your competition. Because at that rate you can attract the best talent and still outperform teams that cost many times more because it takes more people to complete the same tasks. FANG (Facebook, Apple, Netflix, and Google) companies aren't being magnanimous by paying their developers' huge salaries. They are being shrewd and logical. Selecting the best makes them more capable to meet market demand. This book will share strategies for proving you are a better programmer and strategies for positioning yourself as a top talent in the market place. So you can compete for those highly paid positions at top employers.

Each employer will have a different philosophy on employee compensation. Ultimately though there are a few things that dictate how they compete for talent and which band of talent they seek. You need to understand how the business makes money and how your skills can help accelerate their goals.

Entry Level - Two Years Experience?

For most software engineers the toughest job to get is the one right out of college. Employers know that developers right out of college take some time on the job before they hit their stride and can make great software. You will probably see real job postings that say "entry level" two years of experience required. This is employers attempts to keep chumps from cluttering up their resumé inbox. What the job req is saying is do not apply with a blank resumé.

The employment market is a functioning market. The employer wants the best developers just like you want the best tomatoes at the super market. All tomatoes are $2 a pound you are going to pick the best looking tomatoes on display and leave the rest for everyone else. If entry level developers all cost roughly the same, then the company wants the best value. The best value would be someone willing to take an entry-level position who has already built things. So you want to do what you can to make sure you look like the freshest tomato out there. Your resumé needs to showcase your strengths. What problems have you solved? What projects have you built? What makes you better than the other engineers applying for the same position?
You can't expect to be the first tomato picked off the shelf. You may have to interview a few times. The key is to learn

each time and get better. Position yourself as a competent Engineer and there is enough room in the market for you.

The reason the company has a job req out is that they intend to hire someone for that position. If you don't get offered that position then t someone else was probably offered the job. But that's not a bad thing. Now that person you were competing with is no longer available for other jobs. Companies need good people just as much as good people need jobs.

The Developer Career Path

In the software development career field there really is no such thing as a standard career path. The need for great engineers defies rules put in place for other disciplines. In my career, I've met people who landed their first professional position at Developer 2. I've also seen colleagues happily land and stay a developer 3 for over a decade. I've met 24-year-old engineers making well over six figures, and 45-year-old engineers happily making much less than that. Your career will follow any path you set. But in general, this is how most HR departments map out the developer career track.

Software Developer I:

This is an entry-level position. Some job postings may say 2 years of relevant experience and a bachelor's degree.

Software Developer 1 is a junior development position. In general, you will probably be told what you are working on. You will probably be paired up with a mentor or more senior developer who will read your code. One pro tip here, ask to read your mentor's code too. Read their code and learn from it. Ask them why they did things the way they did. If they are any good you will have some good conversations and teaching moments come from you reading their code.

Software Developer 2:

This is still a junior/mid-level position. In general, you can be promoted from a Developer 1 to Developer 2 in one to two years. In the developer 2 positions, chances are you will become a more trusted member of the team. Your team will count on you getting a significant amount of work done. At this point, you should be pulling your weight as a developer. In team meetings, you will probably have a little more leeway in picking the work you will be doing. At this point, if you run into a roadblock you should be able to research or engineer your way around most code related blockers.

Software Developer 3:

This is a mid-level position. In general, most people hit developer 3 sometime around the 3-6 year career mark. This is a rank you can stay in for a long time if you want to. Not everyone moves on to be a Senior Dev, Lead Dev or architect. At Developer 3 you should be pulling your weight on the team, and you may be mentoring a developer 1 or 2. But your main focus is still primarily being an individual contributor to the team.

Senior Developer:

This tends to require about 7-8 years of experience. Senior developers and Dev 3 still spend 90% of their workday coding. It's typical that Senior devs teach techniques from time to time. Senior developers review code for quality and correctness. They probably do some higher level design work, but rarely get involved with meetings and initiatives larger than the development team.

Lead Software Developer:

8-10 years: Lead software developers spend less time coding and more time leading. Lead developers will often teach techniques, and set team standards. They also will act as a liaison between the dev team and management. Leads will be responsible for estimating project timelines and making sure projects are delivered on time and on target. Their focus will still be on the team, helping each team member develop and grow. They will also provide estimates and help set timelines for the team.

Software Architect:

10 years + Software Architects are the trusted technical advisors of the business. While Software Leads focus on the software team; architects tend to focus on the big picture enterprise-wide. They set strategic timelines, standards, and architectures. Architects don't get to do that much coding, most of their time is spent in meetings, creating high-level designs, researching industry trends, creating estimates and project plans.

Developers Make lots of Money

Software Developers make a lot of money. According to the Federal Bureau of Labor Statistics Software Developers made on average $100,690 a year. That is pretty good, the average professional is making six figures. So the above average developer is making quite a bit more than that. That statistic includes everyone in the career so don't expect to start at six figures. If starting above six figures is not entirely unheard of but you will need every penny to pay for your ridiculously high rent and cost of living. According to NACE (National Association of College Employers), the average starting salary for a software developer in 2017 was $66,847. Software developers start out making more than most people make late in their careers in other fields.

Software Engineering job openings are expected to grow roughly 19% over the next 20 years putting even more upward market pressure on salaries. Software developers make a lot of money. Also, there is pressure on the H1B program in the US, which could push salaries even higher. Great software developers, will be able to demand great working conditions, great pay and many perks for the foreseeable future. We are already seeing a trends that lend to better lifestyle and more flexibility like flexible schedules and the ability to work 100% remotely.

According to the Bureau of Labor and statistics, there were 1,114,000 software development jobs in 2014. Software

Development is a growing field because developers can reduce the complexity of many repeatable tasks to the click of a button or have things run automatically on a schedule. Good businesses thrive on predictable repeatable processes. Running software is cheaper and less error-prone than paying people to do manual tasks.

With AI advancing it is becoming possible to program customer support bots and help desk bots. Soon we will have cars and trucks driven by computers. All of these things put pressure on other industries. But for the foreseeable future, humanity will need clever people to develop the next generation of technology.

The software development career field has lots of promise. It can be a very lucrative profession, but it is not for everyone. There are some drawbacks in this career field. You will never know everything there is to know about software development. You will have to constantly keep learning and relearning as technology moves forward. It is a sedentary desk job and you don't move around a lot, so it is easy to get out of shape if you don't stay disciplined and active outside of work. It takes patience and persistence to solve difficult problems. Being a good developer is not easy.

Chapter 2 Action Guide

- In your notebook make a list of the coding projects that would be good stories to tell employers about.

- Identify some of your personal strengths that could be beneficial to employers and differentiate you from all of the other applicants. Write them down in your notebook for reference later.

- Think of 3 companies you admire and consider how they generate revenue. Write down how software plays into generating that predictable revenue.

CHAPTER 3 Preparing

Failure to plan is planning to fail. Preparation is key in helping you differentiate yourself from the other job applicants. Make no mistake about it preparing and applying for jobs the way this book recommends will probably be more work than you were expecting to do to get a job. The extra work sets you above the other people who are also looking for a job. From a hiring manager's point of view, it's always an "either-or" choice between candidates. The candidate that can impress the interviewers the most in the relatively limited time and space of the application and interview process wins. This chapter will help you stack the deck in your favor.

Market Research

You are participating in the Software Developer employment market. Each job pays its market rate. Each employee demands certain compensation. You are part of the supply side of the equation, supplying your skills, expertise and time.

The employer is participating in the demand side of the equation. From the company's perspective, they need to fill a position to strategically grow or replace a lost worker. Supply and demand are what drives salary. If the company demands an expert in an obscure technology and there are only 10 experts in that technology, then those experts can charge a lot of money for their time and skill set. That is until other smart people get wind of how much those guys are making and skill up and start competing for those high demand jobs.

Companies will pay you exactly what it would cost to replace you. Companies aren't being evil. They are just participating in the market. Likewise, as a participant in the job market, you will make more money if you know your true market value and position yourself in a high paying niche.

Take a step back from the job market and look at another type of competitive market. Imagine you are a farmer and you are selling tomatoes at a large farmer's market. There are a few different ways you could sell your tomatoes. One way would be walk up and down the market and note the prices of your competition then set your price in a way that gives you a strategic advantage. There will be competitors that compete on lowest price and competitors that position themselves as a balance between price and value, and then there will be competitors that market themselves as the luxury choice (Heirloom Artisanal Organic Tomatoes). If this is your first job search you may be tempted to position yourself as the lowest price. Think about that strategy before executing. Companies that pay lower than market salaries tend to provide lower quality services, or sell commodities. That can put business driven caps on compensation and limit the creativity and freedom you have at that company. It can be a little bit of a vicious cycle. They hire low priced people, who have less skill, who bring in less revenue which makes the business run tighter. Often when companies underpay their employees it's just one of the ways they mistreat them.

You would be much better off positioning yourself in one of the other two camps, either a balance of value for price or a luxury. If this is your first job and you didn't go to a highly prestigious university, then you should almost certainly go for a balance of value and price. Target companies with solid reputations that pay market rates and position yourself as their dream prospect. You will need to do a little investigating online to find out what they are looking for. And you will need to do some learning and prototyping to prove yourself in the skill sets they are looking for. This work will go a long way in differentiating you from everybody else who applies.

There are a few ways you can go about searching for a job. One way would be to make a list of companies you admire and order that list. Then start at the top of that list and do online research to find out the best way to get an interview. This strategy has some distinct advantages over other ways of going about looking. It is usually a good bet to work for a company you admire. If you admire them, other people do too and this company's name will be on your resumé for a long time. It's the Google alumni affect. Once you work at one prestigious employer you get put to the top of the stack when you apply to other places. The challenge of this strategy is you may need to be creative about breaking through the noise and getting an interview. The common channels are going to be fraught with very talented competition and you may or may not be able to get an interview the traditional way.

Don't be afraid to be creative and try and get in via several alternative routes. You may want to talk to a few recruiters before submitting your resumé directly. Sometimes the recruiter cannot get paid if you submit the resumé through the company's main website. If they can't get paid, they won't be incentivized to help you out. Often companies will work with recruiters to place temp to hire positions exclusively. These kinds of positions are at lower risk to the company and higher risk to the employee. It's easier for the company to end a contractor's engagement than firing a full-time employee. You are free to talk to recruiters, and give them a few weeks to find a position in your dream companies. If they fail at landing you an interview then apply directly on the company's website, or through personal or alumni networks. Many recruiters will ask if you are ok with a contract to hire (temp to hire). This is a personal decision and there are real trade-offs you need to take into account before accepting a contract to hire position.

Contract to hire allows you to work as a contractor with your prospective team during a tryout period. Generally if the team you are working with likes you then they will offer you a full-time position. This type of agreement can effectively get your foot in the door. There are potential drawbacks. While you are a contractor, you are at greater risk of unemployment if the company decides to make any staffing cuts or hiring freezes. Contractors are usually the first ones to feel the pressure of tightened budgets. That being said, you should ask to be compensated for the extra risk you are taking on during any pay rate discussions. When you do a contract to hire there are two salary negotiations. First, there is a negotiation with the contracting firm during your try out period. Then if you are successful you will have another negotiation chance when you become a full-time employee.

Most contracting firms tend to pay via an hourly rate and have very few benefits. Be sure you understand and accept how overtime is handled in your contract. I've seen colleagues in the past not get paid for overtime while they were contracting, and it's because they didn't read their contract and negotiate for paid overtime up front. Most engineering positions are considered "exempt" which means companies may not have to pay you overtime legally unless it's in your contract. It's also important to consider your benefits package. Some contracting companies have bare-bones health plans and a few have 401k plans but they probably aren't as generous as what the regular full-time employees get. Time off is another consideration, be sure to ask about what your PTO allotment will be. Some contracting firms are very generous with time off and others don't provide any.

A second strategy for searching for a job is the online job boards. There are many and the most popular ones are changing constantly. These sites will allow you to search for job listings and post your resumé. When you post your resumé you should also commit to answering your phone as it may start ringing many times a day. Sadly many of the worst recruiters scour these sites and then cold call prospects who post their phone numbers to the sites. You are going to have to screen recruiters just like they are going to try and screen you. The good recruiters should be able to have a conversation about the team looking to do the hiring. This is your full-time job right now so screening phone calls are part of the work you will be doing. Don't waste your time with any recruiters who haven't read your resumé before they call you. They should know and readily be able to answer the hiring managers first name and how long they've been looking to fill the position. If the recruiter can't tell you this kind of information, be professional, but ask them to call you back once they have those answers. This will save you a lot of effort applying for jobs where the recruiter has no existing relationship with the company hiring.

One more strategy is to prove your skills on sites like CodeFights.com and StackOverflow.com. At code fights your coding skills are tested and if you score high enough then you get put in companies recruitment flows. Stack Overflow is a question and answer site and you get points for answering questions. Once you hit a threshold you can put your resumé up for employers to see. Barriers like this keep the riffraff out and make it easier to cut through the noise. It also helps employers prequalify you as someone who is dedicated to your craft.

Depth first searches work best

If there is one thing HR recruiters are good at it's filtering out noise. People who submit 10 resumes in 2 hours will be part of the noise and not have a very high success rate at getting their resume through that first filter. Here are some things to consider when you start your search.

1. Start by Identifying your top 5 employers:
In your job search notebook write down the top 5 places you want to work. For the first few weeks dedicate your search to target only these 5 companies. Follow them online, and learn as much as you can about them.

2. Get someone in the company to submit your resume or recommend you:

If your school has a good alumni network, see if there are any alums at your target companies. Often employees get a bonus for recommending good talent, and the recommended professionals also get to skip the first few steps that filter out most resumes. If you can't find an alumni connection, check developer meetups, open source projects, or even twitter. If you look hard enough you can find someone in the company who can help you put your resume in and get you past the gatekeepers. Some companies will have the employee put your resume in. Others the employee will put your email address in on an internal job site and you will then submit your resume through the public job site. Somewhere on the back end the system does an email match to flag recommended resumes.

Don't give up:
Most companies are huge and it may take a few interviews to find a fit. Each time you are rejected, use that as fuel. People doing hiring really do like to hear things like this. "I really want to work here, I've applied for a few positions so far. And I intend to keep applying here until I can find a way to get my foot in the door. This is my top choice, I can't wait to work here." This is why it's really important you admire the company you are applying for. When you say things like that you really need to mean it.

Sorting Out Job Titles

Job titles mean more to the HR department than they do to developers. What's the difference between the responsibilities of a Front End Software Engineer I and a Front End Web Developer 1 ... Probably not much. But there may be a difference in salary. Let's go over some of the more common names for jobs that are just different flavors of entry-level positions for Computer Science majors just out of university.

Software Engineer 1:

This is pretty generic and could mean just about anything. You will need to read the job requisition to find out which technologies the employer uses. A lot of times they will be asking for 2 years of experience, do your best to explain that you've been making software for over 2
years in university or open source and that requirement won't hold you back.
Software Developer 1:
Just like a Software Engineer 1

Webmaster:

Don't waste your time with this job recs. If they are hiring "webmasters" then you don't want to work for them. They are stuck in the 1990s. Or are looking for someone who's standards are lower than somebody motivated to read this book.

Web Developer 1:

This one can be tricky and honestly, you need to get to know the company doing the hiring to make a judgment. Some companies try to pay a "Web Developer 1" less than say a "Software Engineer 1" but when it gets down to it they are expecting the same skill set and training. Don't be a sucker if the employer doesn't pay market rate you always have the option to walk away. However, some companies just call their junior developers Web Developer 1 and pay well.

Java Software Engineer 1:

You probably learned Java in college. Read the job requisition carefully and see what other technologies and what kind of software you will be building.

Front End Java Engineer 1:

The front end is the part users see. In this position, you will be spending time fighting with user interfaces to make them picture perfect. It can be a headache but also very rewarding. When the app looks awesome you get more credit than the back end engineers.

Back End Java Engineer 1:

Like defense on a soccer team back end engineers tend to get less credit when things go well and more blame when things go wrong. Don't let that dissuade you though. Back end engineers quickly become unit test ninja's and get a lot more exposure to the nitty-gritty engineering problems like caching, protocol translation, multi-threading and such. This is a really good position to learn fast.

<TechnologyX> Developer 1, Junior <TechnologyX>:

There are too many technologies to name. Be careful if the technology is too fringe, it may make the skills you learn on the job less valuable to other future employers. But if you see a new technology catching on, you may want to embrace the opportunity to be an early adopter. If you start a good blog about this technology you could quickly climb to become a nationally recognized expert in your field.

Database Admin 1:

As a database admin, you won't be learning how to make software. You will be keeping databases up and running efficiently. Since many database admin functions are being eaten alive by cloud hosting you may want to consider this opportunity carefully. In 10 years this position will look very different than it does today with recent advances in big data, cloud technologies, and document databases.

System Admin 1:

These guys keep servers up and running. In this job, you will spend a lot of time managing memory, logs and backups. The command line and bash scripting tools will become your best friend. However, like the DBA many of the System Admin functions are being consolidated and simplified via cloud and virtualization/containerization technologies so the admin job is rapidly changing. That being said, there will still be a strong market demand for System Admins going forward. The future is in automating everything so that you can quickly scale up and down based on demand.

.Net Developer 1, Junior .Net Engineer:

.Net engineers work on software that runs on the Microsoft .NET platform which is very similar in capabilities to Java. For some reason, there is a little bit of a rivalry between .Net developers and Java developers. Either way, you go, they are both great technologies. .Net does tend to have more complete documentation since it's managed by Microsoft. Pay tends to be roughly the same.
Front End Web Developer 1, Junior Front End Web Developer: This position probably means you will be writing HTML, CSS, and Javascript. Take a look at the job requisition and pay attention to the frameworks and technology stacks mentioned. There are 1000s of ways you can do web front ends now. And every place's team seems to use a slightly different technology stack. Like the Java and .NET front end developers, you will be making UI's pixel perfect which can be a pain. With pain also comes the reward of being able to show off your work. Having work you can show off, and stories to tell will help your career progress faster.

Node Developer 1:

This could be called Back End Javascript developer but Node sounds way cooler. In this position, you will be writing code that most likely provides services that run a web front end, by connecting some persistent data store to REST web services. Like Java and .NET back end engineers, you will get many opportunities to learn lots of things quickly.

Python Developer:

Similar to everything else but using Python. This language's adoption continues to grow mainly in the big data, and AI fields. These positions could be really valuable. Especially if you can get a position dealing with AI. The profession is going through an AI renaissance and now is a good time to get into this part of our field.

Junior Full Stack Developer:

Full stack developers do it all. They make the front end, then make the services to drive the front end, and then they write the database commands to persist and retrieve data. This is a great opportunity to learn a lot of new skills.

There are a few things to consider when selecting your first job. Going down one path will make it easier to find a job at the next level in that specialty. Java 1 -> Java 2 -> Java 3 etc. But it is possible and will be necessary for you to switch technologies during your career. I started in Java then moved to .NET then Objective C and now I work with predominantly Javascript. Chances are in 5 years you will be working in a completely different technology than what you start in. Once you have one you can learn whatever you want to take your career to the next level.

Early in your career look for jobs that will give you interesting stories to tell. Ideally want the things you work on to be recognizable, respected and valuable. Look for jobs where you can rapidly learn new skills in technologies that are growing in adoption. Look to work
in places where you can use your talent to build things you are proud of.

Train Up

Your college education is very important for a few reasons.

1. It proves you can start something difficult and stick with it until it's complete.

2. It proves you can learn difficult concepts quickly.

3. It teaches you many of the fundamental concepts that will continually show themselves as you progress in your career.

It probably did not show you how to make good software. You will need to start training up immediately to sharpen your software making muscle. You want to work in technologies that are market relevant and you want to build things that you can show off in interviews and meetings with potential employers.

By now you should have gone to a few job searching websites and perused the Software Engineer 1 (And similar job titles) positions. There is probably a list of 3 to 5 technologies that you don't know that continually show up as requirements in these postings. For instance, perusing listings today many require GIT experience. If this is still the case when you are reading this then you need to learn how to get up and running with GIT fast, get the basic understanding and then find a way to demonstrate that competency.

If I needed to learn GIT, I'd first read the documentation on it then do one of the many online courses on it. After that, I'd create a few open source projects on Github and practice doing some branching and merging. I'd even get a few former classmates to join me so we can see how things work when multiple developers work on the same files. All the while we would be working where everyone can see our work. So that I can open up Github on demand and walk an interviewer through the different scenarios and demonstrate that I really can work with GIT.

In an entry-level position, you aren't going to be expected to know everything. You actually won't be expected to know much at all beyond basic problem solving and language proficiency. You will be expected to learn fast, integrate and synthesize information and use that to build things. You need to practice doing this with the hottest technologies today, before you interview.

When you interview, it is important to show the hiring manager that you are the kind of developer that takes personal initiative to go out and learn new things. We all want to work with people we can count on, and the best way to show me I can count on you is by showing me your character, and willingness to learn before I even ask you to learn.

Developer Meet Ups

While you are in college and while you are looking for a job you should be going to developer meet-ups for a multitude of reasons. Here are the top reasons you need to carve out time in your schedule to go eat free pizza and hear people talk about tech.

1. You get to eat free pizza and hear people talk about tech. If you don't enjoy these things you should probably rethink your career aspirations. Seriously though, you will learn something new, and that will make you more valuable when the time comes to find employment.

2. Companies and recruiters are there to identify and entice top talent. By going where people are self-selecting to learn and improve themselves you are in effect doing all the hard work for the recruiter and separating the wheat from the chaff. By being at the meet up you distinguish yourself as a cut above your peers who didn't show up. Being present and participating could speed up your job searching process.

3. The people you meet will be from the entire spectrum of the career ladder. You will see senior developers down to

junior and student developers. These people are your people. Ask for their advice on how they ended up where they are. They may know of an opening or a position you may be interested in.

4. Above all be courteous and warm to the people you meet. You may find them on the other side of the interview one day interviewing you. If you do be sure to mention that you met them at the meetup. The best advantage you can have going into a job interview is the interviewer already being familiar with you and having a favorable impression of your work ethic.

Meetups are great for your career, and you should keep at them even after you land your first job. They are a great way to expand your horizons and keep a pulse on how the technology world is changing. The relationships you generate will help propel your career as you grow.

Leverage Open Source

Open source provides a loophole around the not so mandatory "2 Years of Experience" line in most entry-level Software jobs. Open source is great because it's open you don't have to have an employer hire you to start getting "professional" credit. So get on Github today and make an account and go do a few tutorials this week. Issue a few pull requests! Congratulations, the timer just started on your professional coding career. Contribute regularly and you have real social proof you can make things.

Pick what you learn:

You can work on anything you want. No one is going to tell you no. Want to learn Node.js, then do it, and check in your code to an open source repository. Want to learn Java and the Spring framework, set up a project and check it in. You can learn anything you want and demonstrate mastery with open source. This is the proof employers are looking for when they are hiring.

Show what you are learning. Using open source regularly will help you and future employers see what you've worked on. It also allows employers to take a look at your growth rate. They can send an engineer to look through your portfolio and see how your code improves as you grow in your coding skills. Build a portfolio of technologies and projects that is easy to share with employers.

Open source lets you showcase your consistency and passion. This separates the professionals from the amateurs. As a hiring manager if I go to a prospects Github contributions graphic and see a lot of green there is a really good chance I will extend them an offer. It shows they are consistent and active. It separates the wheat from the chaff.

Creating Your Portfolio

I recommend bringing a printed version of your portfolio. When you get into the interview any number of things can go wrong with cell service and you may not be able to show off your work via a phone or tablet. Having your portfolio printed and ready will be a huge help in showing that you are the kind of person who takes things seriously. Heres the list of things I recommend preparing in your portfolio.

1. A cover letter, addressed to the interviewer if possible. The cover letter techniques are discussed in other places in this book.

2. An up to date resumé

3. An index of projects and things you've made, either on your own or in school.

4. An executive summary page for each project. Your executive summary should have a screenshot, and a two or three sentence description of what you made and the key technologies used to make it.

5. Some sample code from the project. You don't need all of it, just some snippets. Be sure to include some snippets from your unit test files.

6. Some class diagrams or data flow diagrams and pretty charts are always nice too.

Print it all out with a cover page and buy a nicer binder to collate it all together. You want it to be sturdy and look professional. You want it to look like it took time and effort to put together. The effort sets you apart.

At the end of the interview offer to leave the portfolio with the interviewer. You want to leave it with either the hiring manager or the technical lead after the interview. This will give them something to discuss after you leave.

Having a real portfolio like this shows the interviewing team more than you can imagine. Primarily it shows that you do work you are proud to show others. Secondly, it shows you understand what the employer is looking for and have empathy for their needs as they are searching to fill the position. Not to mention it proves that you take initiative and come prepared. Making, printing and bringing a portfolio is going to give you a distinct advantage over all other job applicants.

Breaking through the Noise

The world today has a lot of noise. We are constantly connected, constantly getting more information than our animal brains have had time to adapt to digest. Most of the data our brains ingest is instantly discarded. Truly reaching and getting a hold of someone is a very difficult task. Don't believe me? Who did you listen to yesterday? Try making a list. How many real conversations did you have yesterday that you can remember today?

I can count on one hand the conversations from yesterday that I remember today. The rest was noise. What were the differences between the conversations that were noise and the ones that stuck with you? Doing some self- examination, I see a trend. I tune into people I want to emulate. I listen to people who genuinely care for me. I cared because they cared about me.

Here are a few things I think can help you break through the noise and better reach those around you.

1. Care for yourself. This sounds like a weird thing to mention when talking about how to better reach others, but self-care matters. People are attracted to and tune into healthy people. Sir Richard Branson is famous for saying that the most important thing he does every day is exercise.

2. Care for other people. People don't care about what you have to say until they are certain you care about them.

3. Practice gratitude. Expressing gratitude to those around you creates dopamine responses to both the person expressing gratitude and the person receiving gratitude. Dopamine is the bonding neurotransmitter.

Here's how you can apply these three practices in the context of a job search. Make sure you set your alarm clock every morning. Set a morning routine that includes breakfast, meditation, and exercise. Make sure you take care of your hygiene and stay well groomed. All this will have a subconscious effect on the quality of the work you will be doing to land your next job. When you are healthy it is reflected in all that you do. Conversely, if you are not healthy then you will be working from a disadvantaged position.

Caring for other people in the context of a job search means understanding the perspectives of the people on the other side of the table. That is why at the beginning of the book we dedicated so much time to the people involved and the motivations they have in this process. Anticipate the recruiter's needs and come prepared for them. Anticipate the hiring manager's concerns and address them before they even ask. Above all show respect and acknowledge that you are working with people. They work for a company, but most importantly they are people. Do what you can to make their work easier. Empathy is a characteristic that is in short supply in today's job market and it can be a key differentiating factor that sets you apart from your competition.

Expressing gratitude is important. Candidates hardly ever send thank you cards to managers and recruiters after interviews. Some feel that putting in the extra effort is cheesy. It only feels cheesy on the receiving end if the thank you cards are impersonal and insincere. You should be writing thank you cards. In the cards, you should include a short but sincere note of gratitude. Something like the following.

Dear John,
Thanks for interviewing me on Tuesday. CompanyX sounds interesting. I appreciated your candor when you spoke about

the more difficult parts of your job. In my job search, I've found that the level of openness unique. I look forward to working on a team with that kind of openness.
Thanks, Your Name

Notice the note took time to identify something unique about the interviewer. Calling out other people's differentiating factors is one of the best ways to get them to recognize yours.

There is a great deal of noise in the world we are living in. You must be deliberate to create traction. Breaking through the noise requires being authentic and caring. It takes deliberate work, but it is by no means rocket science. You already have all the tools you need to break through the noise and create impact. Take care of yourself. Care for the people around you. And find things to be thankful for.

Chapter 3 Action Guide

1. Spend an afternoon looking at job sites online. Dice.com, LinkedIn, Monster.com are a few. Write down key technologies that tend to be mentioned a lot.
2.Take some time for reflection and then write down your top 5 employers list.
For each one mine your contacts to see if you know anyone already working for those companies.
Take a look at the jobs posted on their corporate website. (Don't apply yet, you want to be prepared first)

1. Start learning some of the technologies you found in your search in step 1. above. Learn in public, by pushing code examples to public repositories on Github or Bitbucket.

2. Go to Meetup.com and see if you can find meetups related to the technologies you are learning. Go to the meetups, arrive early and stay late. Talk to as many people as possible.

3. Start curating your professional portfolio. You want to fill it with examples of work that you are proud of, and can fully explain.

CHAPTER 4 Understand Your Audience

Your professors in school may have touched on this. Especially if you took a public speaking class. It's amazing to me the number of absolutely brilliant engineers I've worked with who forget about their audience when communicating. You come at the world from an entirely different perspective than anyone else. Most people don't know the difference between a stack trace from a for loop. To be able to communicate and reach other people you must connect with them. Connecting with them requires knowing their perspective. This chapter explores three different audiences, all of which you must understand to put your best foot forward while job searching.

The Company's Perspective

Why do companies hire software developers? Why do companies hire anybody? The answers to these questions are different for every company. And the answers dictate how you will be treated in the company after you get hired. The only reason a company will hire a person is it believes it will make its owners more money. Think about that for a second and let that sink in. The only reason any company will hire for any position is that it believes it will make more money after making the hire than if they didn't hire anyone at all.

Smaller companies tend to hire one at a time, larger companies may hire in batches. If the company is hiring in batches, there is a good chance for the project that batch is getting put to work on has a pretty high Return On Investment (ROI) for the company. In any case, it's important to understand that if you plan to stay at any company for any period you need to play a role in the company where they make more money with you than without you. Fortunately, this is pretty easy for software engineers which is why there is a high demand for our skills. Software developers can write a program that runs 24 - 7 and the only cost to the company after its built is the cost of improvements and electricity.

As you progress in your job search study the companies you are interested in. How do they make money? Why would having people like you help them make more money for their owners or shareholders? Is the role you would play essential to the core operating model of the company? Or would you be in a support position? In my experience, the higher paychecks and exciting opportunities lie in the positions of the core of the company's operating model. It makes sense too, the core of the company is how it makes money. Everything else may be required but at some point will be viewed as less important than the companies core competency. How do you know if something is part of the company's core competency? Simply determine how the project you will be working on impacts the company's customer base. If customers would care then you are working on core software, otherwise, you are working on something else. There are still good jobs outside the core of the business, but as a rule, promotions will come slower, and budget cuts will hit earlier.

It is important to consider the age and stage of the company. Startups tend to be riskier, and risks should come the potential for reward. Fortune 500 companies tend to be more stable, but also tend to be more controlled by process and political factions like HR. In a company that's growing quickly, you could go from the junior developer to the senior guy mentoring 5 developers in a year or two. That kind of growth could be an excellent opportunity. On the other hand, in a big company, you can probably find a mentor who has been making software since you were born. Honestly, if you can find a mentor like that do anything you can to grow that relationship. The wisdom you will get out of that will pay greater dividends than your college degree.

Human Resource's Perspective

Depending on the size of the company you may or may not have to deal with getting past the company's Human Resources group (HR). The experience I've had with really large companies, the hiring side of HR is heavily augmented with contractors. Hiring tends to come in waves and when the company is in a growth phase the company can usually scale up hiring faster by signing a contract with an outside vendor to bring in talent. HR cannot hire you, but they can keep you from being hired.

The way it usually works is the manager that needs more workers (aka the hiring manager) requests a job requisition. If this gets approved by middle / upper management and then the requisition gets sent to HR. The Job Requisition (aka Job Req) is an order form for what the perfect employee looks like. It's got fields like the title for the position, years of experience needed, skills needed, and technologies the applicant should know. HR usually looks over the job req and ensures that the hiring manager didn't leave out any required fields, (ex. Years of Experience Required, Bachelors/Masters Required, etc). The people in HR are people specialists and not technology specialists, so they will not generally know the difference between Perl and Python.

One of the key things you need to know about HR is that they will probably screen your resumé before the hiring manager ever gets a chance to see it. You can count on them checking your resumé for spelling and grammar. Also, you can count on them looking for keyword matches. The HR professional will go through a stack of resumés and narrow the field down to what they believe is the best 5 or so applications to forward to the hiring manager. This is critical, for your resumé to even get to the hiring manager it must have good spelling and grammar. It also must be readable by someone outside of the software engineering field.

Companies pay consultancies large sums of money to get the going rates for positions. HR takes this data and then sets up compensation rules and ranges for how they compensate for each position. The larger the company, the more formal and rigid the process. The point to take away here is that when you are eventually offered a position, the salary offered will probably in the low/middle area of the range that HR has set for that position. The hiring manager may have some wiggle room in increasing the offer if she wants you on her team.

Negotiating is uncomfortable but necessary. 15 minutes of awkward negotiation could earn you a few extra thousand dollars a year. Chapter 7 will talk more about negotiation. From HR's perspective, their job is to protect the company from legal risk and make sure the company follows the sometimes complicated hiring laws. They also serve as a filter for the hiring manager, to screen applicants, set up interviews and answer the phone when applicants call about job application status. Finally, they set the ranges of salaries as discussed earlier.

Hiring Manager's Perspective

The hiring manager is the guy who will be your boss if you get hired. In many ways, this should be the most straight forward point of view to understand. Put yourself in the shoes of the guy doing the hiring. What would you look for in an interviewee? What would you look for in a new employee? Your job in this relationship is to provide what the hiring manager is looking for.

With developer jobs, many recent college grads feel like they are still completely unqualified for any development position. Chances are in college you never really built a complete software application that is usable by a member of the general public. People who have been making software for a long time get that it is not easy. Nobody who knows software development will say making software is easy. So if the position being hired for isn't required to be knowledgable about everything software what then, do they need to show?

1: An excitement for the mission of the company. If you aren't at least excited about the software you will be working on, you should work somewhere else. Software is too boring, and difficult to build if you aren't interested in what you are building. Your work will be crap, and it will show. And that will affect your career, in a downward vicious cycle. So, before you apply, determine if you can be excited about what is being built and display that excitement during your interview and on follow up calls.

2: Don't be a jerk. If you are a jerk, you won't get hired. Nobody wants to work with jerks.

3: Show that you study, learn, and create on your own time too. While anyone can be taught to make things. There is something inherent in the 10x group of makers that drives them to constantly be creating.

4: Be curious. Ask questions about how things work. Ask about motivations for why they decided on technology X over framework Y. Your curiosity shows that you are excited, it shows that you want to see how it all works. These are traits that go far for young developers.

5: Ask to be on the team: It sounds obvious, but not everyone asks. At the end of your interview ask to be on the team. Looking back on the dozens of interviews I've done, the applicants who wrapped up with a simple. "I had a great time meeting you today. I would love to be a part of this team. " ended up getting offers at the end of the day.

Chapter 4 Action Guide

1. For each of the companies on your list take some time to list out some attributes you think the company, HR department, hiring manager would be specifically looking for in a candidate.

2. Schedule tasks and the time to do those tasks to improve the attributes you listed above.

CHAPTER 5 Applying

This part of the job search is the meticulous part. This is where most people go wrong, so it's your opportunity to turn this gate into a strategic advantage. Set aside at least 2 full hours for every position you apply for. When you decide to apply for a position first read the job requisition completely. If there are terms in the requisition you don't understand go do some web searches to figure them out. If the job still sounds like one you are interested in sit down and get to work.

Customizing Your Resume

As you are going through this process, visualize that the hiring manager for this position is sitting right across the table from you. We want everything you put into the application system to be customized specifically for that person. So to start you need to fully customize your resume to highlight the skills you've been acquiring in the very same technologies the Job Req mentions. There should be some overlap from the technologies you've been learning from the preparation chapter and the meetups you've been going to. Use the exact keywords found in the job rec. The first filter you need to pass is the HR professional. They are going to try and match the words on your resume to the words in the job rec, and they may not know that REST API's are a kind of "Service

Architecture" so if the job posting says familiarity with "Service Architectures" and you know REST. You could say something like ->
REST Service Architectures: Proficient in REST Patterns, design, definition, and usage, see my GitHub here for some examples I've provided. http://github.com/ <MyRESTExampleRepo>

Let's break that down. First, it shows that you know what Service Architectures are for any technical person, but it also satisfies the keyword for HR. Then you follow up with verifiable proof. When you do this sort of thing, for many of the key skills they are looking for, you are going to stand out.

For each skill use terms like "Familiar, Proficient, Capable" as you describe your ability with each tool or technology. Don't oversell yourself but don't undersell either. If you've built something that works with technology and understands it enough that you can modify it to make it do what you want then most people would be fine considering that "Familiar".

Provide as much proof as you can via links to example work. This goes a long way in showing initiative and expertise. Use spell check and proofread your resume. HR usually has permission to discard resumes with spelling errors. A simple misspelling can be something that could end up eliminating you if the team only has time for a few interviews.

When your resume is ready it should be completely customized for the job req you are applying for. It should have lots of links to prove you can do what you say you can. It should be easy to read and free from spelling and grammatical errors. Next, you need to create a custom cover letter. Once you have it created to save it in two formats, one as a plain text file and another as a pdf. Some older HR resume sites do best parsing text files. But you want the actual file they print out for interviewers to be formatted in a way that can't get messed up by the back end system. PDFs keep your resume formatted correctly for the humans who will be reading your resume.

Your Cover Letter

Your cover letter is your chance to tell your story and give the recruiter and hiring manager the context beyond your qualifications. This is an opportunity to tailor your story and customize it for this employer. Don't waste this opportunity by posting a boilerplate cover letter. Spend time on writing a custom one for each application. There are only a few ways you can distance yourself from the crowd and having a truly custom cover letter is key.

If you have a contact on the inside write them their custom cover letter and send it to them directly with a PDF copy of your resume. You want to make it as easy as possible for your contact inside the company to make you look great. Arm them with everything they need to go make the case to get you the interview.

Open your cover letter with a sentence that is both memorable and thoughtful. You want to draw the reader in and signal that this isn't a form letter in the first line. Make sure someone reading knows you thought carefully about what to say and that you are highly motivated to get to work with them.

Spend the following paragraphs, explaining what you intend to deliver for the company. Obviously the more you know about the position the more specific you can be in calling out what you intend to do in your first few months as an employee. When you can, call out relevant experiences either in school, internships or other jobs that can be applied in the new job.

Finally, close by asking for an interview. End with a strong call to action, the goal of the letter is to get you a conversation with the hiring manager. Be direct, and ask for the interview.

Chapter 5 Action Guide

1.For each job you are applying to create a custom resume, tailored to the positions posting, using as many of the words as you can in the posting itself.

2.For each job you are applying to create a custom cover letter that quickly sets you apart, and tells the story of how your skills will uniquely benefit this company.

CHAPTER 6 Consider Recruiters

There is so much demand for good talent in the industry that there now is a sub-industry of technical recruiters. They can be a great ally in your job search. For one thing, they know the market, and what employers are paying for certain skill sets, and they are incentivized to get you at least the average market rate. The average is better than half of your peers will get for their first developer positions. Recruiting agencies generally get some percentage of commission based on the starting salary of the placement. For instance, if the placement commission is 15% then the recruiter's company will get paid $7500 for placing you. Most recruiting firms focus on mid and senior developer placements, however, it's still worth adding some recruiters to your network. You can probably find some by mentioning on LinkedIn that you are starting your career as a software engineer could use any help finding meaningful work.

Once you do get a recruiter's name and an email address, schedule a phone call. On the call give them an overview of what you are looking for, and ask for their advice. At the end of the conversation, thank them for the advice and ask them to coffee. If they accept the coffee meeting will set you apart from other candidates and signal that you are highly motivated. If they turn you down, don't let that stop you. Recruiters are busy too and they make money by placing people. Some only focus on more experienced candidates. It may take calling many different recruiters to get some interest. It's also important to know that you can work with more than one recruiter at once. When you do get coffee meetings to come prepared with a printed portfolio of your work, share the highlights and be sure to pay for their lunch. This should earn you some allies in your search. The more people looking to place you the better.

The business model of the recruiter is a lot like that of a real-estate agent. Instead of selling houses they are placing people. Relationships are important, you will need help as your career progresses. You should do your best to keep in touch with recruiters so that down the road you can jump to a different employer to ensure your compensation stays at the market rate. Employers are never incentivized to pay you more, and you have the most leverage for a raise when you switch companies or have the ability to get offers from other companies. Recruiters will help you find open doors when you need to make your next switch. It is of paramount importance that you treat them with respect and honesty during and after your search. Too many developers end up not being forthcoming with recruiters and play them as pawns. While this strategy may work out in the short term, in the long term your reputation could be damaged. This isn't going to be your last job search and the software development world is smaller than you think. Treat everyone as you hope to be treated.

Expect the same treatment from recruiters and hold them accountable if they are not forthcoming with you as well. By following the patterns and practices in this book you should be positioning yourself as top tier talent. And in this employment market, Top Tier talent is extremely valuable.

CHAPTER 7 A Good Employer

Ultimately a good employer is one that has interesting work and pays you fairly for that work. A job at a great employer is more important than the salary you receive. There is no denying that money is important, so are some other factors. Does the company do something you admire?

It's hard to put your heart into your work when you ultimately don't admire the things that the company does. It will be hard to perform above the level of your peers and rise in the ranks if you don't like what your company does.

Is the company growing or shrinking?

You will find more opportunities and less stress in a growing company. Shrinking companies will have less money for training, and fewer people to do the things the company needs to be done. It's best to join a growing company.
Are the company's competitors growing or shrinking?
It's even better to join a growing company in a growing industry because that means companies like yours will be needing your skills. Increased demand raises the salary you can command.

It's good to look more closely at your prospective employers and look for signs things may not be going as smoothly as you think. Here are a few things to look out for.

The companies that pay less also tend to treat their employees worse as well. To the number, the companies that I've worked for that were known for paying well also treated their employees well in other ways too. It makes sense too, from the company's perspective people may be a strategic asset or just a cost of doing business. The tricky part is all companies will tell you that their people are their most important asset. How can you tell who's blowing smoke? Pay is one indicator. Another is the longevity of employees on the team. In your interview ask the interviewers how long they've been with the company and if theirs been much turnover. Good companies do have people there who have been there for longer than 2 years. Not so good companies will have retention issues and most people will move on after two years.

Ask the interviewers how much overtime is typical. If you accept the job you will be expected to do the same over time after you get hired. Depending on the project this could be a good or bad thing. One of the best ways to bond with a team is to help them get through a hard time. But be aware of what you are getting into.

What you will be working on matters immensely. You want to work on projects that are part of the strategic heart of your employer. If possible you want to be on the system that is the core competency of the company. Those projects never have funding issues. They get all the glory and bonuses when things go well, and they get extra funds to hire when things get rough. You are also collecting stories for your interviews later in your career. Working on exciting projects will make those interviews go much better. To the extent that you can, you want to work on projects that are visible outside the company you will be working on. Not only will that mean you

get more visibility, but you can also show future employers
what you worked on.

CHAPTER 8 Acing The Interview

If you've read up to this point and done the things mentioned earlier then the interview will just be a formality for you. All you need to do now is show up on time and walk the interview team through all of the things you've prepared. They've been looking for you. Today is your chance to show them that you understand what they are looking for and how you will deliver.

Screening Calls

Most companies do screening calls before flying a candidate out or bringing them into the office for an in- person interview. They do this because it's cheaper and easier than handling the logistics for meeting someone in person when it may not work out. At this stage, HR has already qualified your resumé and passed it on the hiring manager. Your resumé has done its job. You could be the only one being screened for the position or there may be a few people getting calls today. But don't fret. You're more prepared for this because you've done the preparation work up front.

For the actual call, you want to be in a quiet place with good phone reception in front of a computer with a good internet connection. You want to be able to send or receive an email to the interviewer if needed. And there may or may not be a screen share. Clear your desk ahead of time and have your portfolio ready to share.

Screening calls tend to be more technical. Expect the interviewer to ask you both technical questions and non-technical questions. Be direct, you aren't expected to know every answer. However, there are good ways and bad ways to show you don't know anything. I've found one of the best approaches when you don't know is answering with something like this.

"I'm not sure I'm familiar with what you are asking. I don't think I know the answer. Can you help me understand? " When the interviewer responds he will probably teach you something. If you can this is a great time to relate it to other concepts you do know, and how you've used those other concepts in your open source, or portfolio work. Keep in mind the real questions underneath every other question are. Is this person competent? And is this person someone I can work with. If you can convey competence and camaraderie than increase your chances of success.

There are a few things you need to be prepared to answer, and it's best you think about these things and jot them down ahead of time.

"Tell us a little about yourself" this is almost always the first question in interviews. Your goal is to sound interesting and inquisitive, spend longer than 15 seconds responding but no longer than a minute. This is your chance to mention anything that may be relevant that would make you stand out to the interviewers. At the end of the interview, it's a good thing if you are "The guy who mentioned his app in the app store" or "The woman who contributes to that open source project." Give the interviewers a vignette that will stick with them.

"Do you have any questions for us?" This one almost always comes towards the end of the screening. Your goal is to get to the next step, so I don't recommend asking controversial questions at this stage. Questions like "What should I be learning between now and when I get started to start well?" and "What's the best part about working here?"

Preparing For The In- Person Interview

If you get past the screening the next step is most often an in person or more in-depth interview. For this one, you are going to want to make sure you dress appropriately. Proper attire is tricky and highly dependent on the company you are interviewing with. If it's a bank or a high powered consultancy, a fancy suit is appropriate. If it's a small agency or a startup, you may need more relaxed attire. I'd recommend googling, "What's the best attire for interviewing at <company name>" chance are you aren't the first person to have this question. When in doubt, it's almost always better to go a little overdressed than underdressed. I've been in interviews where the candidate disqualifies himself for being dressed too casually. I've never been a part of an interview where the candidate was penalized for being too dressed up. If you do wear a suit and everyone else is in flip-flops, you should address that in the interview. You are being assessed for cultural fit, and what you wear does have some influence on that assessment. So if you are in a fancy suit and everyone is in flip-flops. A quick joke about how everyone is going to call you a suite guy and how you are jealous you didn't wear flip-flops today can go a long way to answering that cultural fit question.

Before you go to the interview prepare a copy of your portfolio. Print things out on nice paper, make it look professional. When you leave, leave it with the person who appears to be the leader. You want to look like the most prepared person they interview this year. And this is your chance to shine.

The Interview From The Other Side Of The Table

When I'm interviewing you for a job there are only 2 questions I'm trying to answer. I may ask you many other questions but they are all questions to determine the answers to these two main questions. If you fail to convince me of these two things I'll keep looking for other people to fill the position.

1. Can you help me make good software?
2. Are you the kind of person I want to work with?

Notice that there are a few things that never enter my decision making calculus during the interview. You aren't being compared to anyone else at this point. You got to the in-person interview, and I'm not usually going to schedule in-person interviews with two people ahead of time for one position because if I like the first one, I'm going to want to make an offer immediately. Then I'd have to call back the guy with the next interview and say sorry pal, we already found someone. If you are at an in-person interview then the chances are that the job is yours to lose.

Also, notice that I'm not even thinking about money at this point. And there are a couple of reasons for this. It's not my money it's the company's, I don't care if you make 10k more or less than what you expect to make. I care about how working with you will affect my life. Will I have to stay late to fix your screw ups because you are the kind of person who doesn't dot your i's and crosses your t's? Are you a sarcastic jerk that I'm going to have to constantly be careful around? Do you have a sense of humor? Are you secure enough to say "I don't know" when you don't know something? I want to enjoy the people I work with and convincing me that you are easy to be around is half of the interview.

The other half is competence. Can you help the team? Software Developers that can't write software are worse than having an empty position on the team roster. They are a dead weight that holds the whole team back. If I have someone who can't code and can't learn on their own, I either need to stop what I'm doing and teach them, or do my work quickly then follow up with them and hold their hand while they do their work with me. Keeping incompetent people off of my team roster is my number one priority. My teammates are counting on my judgment, and when I mess up and let incompetence on the team I take serious credibility hit. You can prove you are competent to me by coming prepared, anticipating my questions, and speaking Intelligently about the things you made in your portfolio.

The most important thing to remember is that I'm secretly cheering for you as you interview. I want you to be a fit for my team so I can stop doing these stupid interviews and get back to making cool software. When you come fully prepared, and relaxed, open to talking shop, you'll get the job.

In Person Interview

Congratulations you are winning the game. No matter what today will be a success either you will interview well and get the job or you will learn more about yourself and the process to be better at this next time. Either way, you are winning. You've done a lot of work to prepare for this, and that gives you an advantage over your competition. Let's talk about how to prepare for this crucial step. And what you will be up against.

The days or weeks before your interview make sure your interview attire is good to go. If it needs to be cleaned and pressed send it to the cleaners and get that taken care of. You should be dressing in full business attire. Men that means a suit and a tie, unless you are applying to a startup or the person setting up the interview tells you what to wear. You need to look clean, healthy, professional and confident.

The night before your interview gets a good night's sleep, don't drink or go out partying, you need to look and feel your best. Set two alarms so you can be sure to wake up on time and have plenty of time for preparation. Start the day with a good hearty breakfast. Don't drink too much coffee. You will naturally be amped up a little on adrenaline, so you probably don't need to add any extra uppers. If you can fit it in, getting a light exercise session can help you get loose before suiting up and getting to the interview.

Make sure you bring your work portfolio and a notebook and pen. If you can show off your work via a tablet, you may want to bring that along too. The key is to come in just a little more prepared than everyone else. You've prepared for this, and now it's just a few introductions and conversations to share the work you've been doing.

Before the interview, while you are waiting, take some deep breaths. You are going to do just fine. When the interview starts to focus on the people interviewing you, ask them questions that show you are interested in them and the topics, they bring up. Answer the questions directly. When you don't know something admit to it and ask questions that show you are interested in the answer. Above all be present. At this stage of the game, you are one of the finalists, probably the only finalist. Often at this stage, they are just screening to see if they can work with you. Are you a cultural fit? Meaning would the interviewer feel comfortable having you on their team solving problems with them every day.

Don't expect it to go smoothly. Some interviewers will either challenge you or be abrasive on purpose to see how you handle stress. As long as you stay open, honest and candid you will be fine. Most interviewers are subconsciously interviewing you to ensure you aren't a Jerk. Relax, and smile when things get intense. I've even seen interviewees crack a joke when an interviewer gets abrasive. After we told him he was wrong on something that he was right about to see how he'd respond he said something like "Wow you guys are intense, I love this! Let me explain how I see it." From there he calmly went over the things we told him and how he came to his conclusions. He ended up getting an offer.

There are usually two questions you can count on being asked. The first is usually some variation of "Tell us about yourself". The key to this question is to sound like an interesting person that would be nice to work with and finish answering in under a minute. The second question you can expect usually comes towards the end of the interview. "Do you have any questions for us?" A good answer to this is "What is the best part about working here?". Whatever you answer you probably don't want to ask about time off right now, or how negotiable they are on salary, that can be done at a later time. Remember they are judging for cultural fit, so do your best to let them speak about things they are proud of.

Questions that recognize the interviewers have been in your position before are great too. "When you interviewed here, what was the hardest thing to learn as the new guy?". "What technology are you most excited about these days?" Those kinds of questions are great. People want to work with other curious people so ask at least one or two good questions. Your mission for the interview is to convince the people interviewing you that they want to hire you. People tend to say that the interview is a two-way affair. You are interviewing the employer just as much as they are interviewing you. That is true. However, you want an offer regardless of whether you want to work there or not. Having multiple offers will give you negotiating leverage with other employers. So even if the employer sounds like the worst place in the world to work, keep your cool and interview well. You want the offer, even if you never plan on taking the job.

When the interview concludes after you leave the building be sure to write down the names of everyone you met that day and something they spoke about. Your homework is to go and write 3 thank you notes. One for the decision maker, one for the alpha developer in the group and one for the HR person. This is why you need to write to these three people. You should write to the decision maker because they are going to be your boss. The alpha developer is going to be the guy who decides on whether or not to hire you because the boss is going to check with him and take his advice. The HR person or the person who greets you is also very important because chances are they are going to be the one helping you onboard the first few days when you start.

Chapter 8 Action Guide

1. Ensure you have your portfolio printed out, coallated and ready to show off.
2. Make sure your online portfolio is active, public and fully operational so you can bring it up during the interview, if a relevant topic comes up.
3. Store key links on your phone so you can show off your work in the interview if needed.

CHAPTER 9 Negotiating Salary

It is in your best interest to attempt to negotiate salary. This may be the one time in your career where you have the least amount of leverage. Still, I recommend you try and negotiate a salary. 5 minutes of awkward negotiation could easily earn you a $2000 signing bonus or an even about $5000 more in annual compensation. There are very few downsides to asking for more money.

Take a look at this from the hiring manager's perspective. They've been through all the paperwork of setting up a job rec. They reviewed resumés, they've screened applicants on the phone, then they probably paid to fly you in to interview you in person. The whole team agrees you are a good fit. Now if they don't hire you the company is out the amount they spent flying you out. And that would reflect badly on thier negotiating skills as a manager. On top of that, while they care about the company's money. Your salary doesn't come out of their paycheck. So if you ask for more money, they may be inclined to give it to you if they are authorized. In most companies managers do have some wiggle room. Even if they are not authorized and my boss says the offer is final, they will still give you a chance to take the job at what was previously offered. The only thing it costs you is the 5 minutes of awkward negotiation silence.

For fun let's do the math, let's say negotiating gets you an extra $1000 signing bonus and the conversation took 5 minutes. That's $200 a minute, or $12000 an hour for your negotiating time. You only get a few times in your career where you can get paid so much for so little. Seize the awkwardness and ask for more money, you just might get it.

Understand The Other Side

This varies from company to company and can be influenced by several different factors. It's important to understand the companies perspective so you can better understand the motivations of the people on the other side of the table.

The way the company you are interviewing is making money matters. Companies are in business to make money. And you want your future employer to stay in business. Before you join up you should have a solid understanding of how they serve their customers and how they generate revenue. An insurance company is going to compensate employees differently than a rapidly growing start-up company, and a defense contractor is going to have a different compensation model than a boutique software shop.

The rate that the company is growing matters. Faster growing companies need to hire faster and so they may be more motivated to pay a little more. If you are in a fast- growing company, you won't be the newest person on the team for long, and it may be easier to move up the ranks. As a whole its better for your career to be a part of a growing company than it would be to join a shrinking one.

How you are perceived vs. the available talent on the market place matters. If the hiring manager wants you on their team they will do what they can to make an attractive offer. First impressions matter, and interviewing well really can mean extra money.

Most companies have guidelines set up by HR that help managers set the salary. Unfortunately for entry-level personnel, the guidelines are usually the most prescriptive. Unless you have multiple offers, with many employers you won't have much leverage during the salary negotiations. With that in mind, there are no tangible downsides to negotiating salary. You lose if you don't ask for more money.

You may win more money if you ask for it. The worst thing that could happen would be the company you are negotiating with says sorry we can't go any higher, and then you can take the offer you were originally extended.

The Negotiation

Preparation:

In your first set of salary negotiations, you are as close to a commodity as you will ever be. You are fresh out of college just like pretty much everyone else. So you don't have a lot of leverage unless you've happened to get two offers at the same time. As you progress down the career path the problems you solve and the stories you gather will help you differentiate yourself from other software makers. But for now, you probably are just like everyone else you are competing with. Odds are you may not earn much in salary negotiations. However, there is no downside to attempting to negotiate so you certainly should.

What if they retract the offer if you try to negotiate?

If they do that, then you probably don't want to work at that company anyway. It is reasonable to expect a promising candidate to politely attempt to negotiate salary. If they are offended that you negotiate this could be a sign that the company is toxic and probably not a good place to be at anyway.

The work you've put in may pay dividends here.

If you work your job search and network vigorously you may be able to set yourself up for the awesome situation where you get to pick between two or more offers at the same time. In this position as long as you are careful, you have leverage. You can walk away from one deal and take the other, this freedom gives you the advantage of being able to be a little more aggressive in negotiations.

Don't go into negotiations with the mindset that there are winners and losers. Instead, it is more advantageous to go in with the mindset that both sides want to work together and you are just working out the particulars before you start work. Look for places where you can give in that are of high value to the employer. Are you willing to start next week? Does the employer have a big project kick off next week? Then offering to start next week may be a valuable proposition.

It's really important you listen closely during all your interactions with the employer so that you can identify and understand opportunities that you can use for these kinds of propositions.

What are some things the employer can give that are valuable to you that cost them very little? Are you interested in being mentored? Request that you are formally assigned a mentor in your first week when you make the offer of starting early so that you can be present for the project kick-off. During salary negotiation always ask for something when you offer to give something in return. Here is a short list of things you can ask for during salary negotiations.

Money Related: Higher starting salary:

Salary compounds throughout your career. Companies often give out bonuses and raise as percentages of your base salary, so getting this number high early in your career will have a compounding effect as time progresses.

Signing Bonus:

Singing bonuses are great because they give you money right away with very little paperwork or strings attached. Most of the time signing bonuses do come with an agreement that you will stay with the company hiring you for a year or two.

Depending on the paperwork you sign if you take a signing bonus and leave before your allotted period you may have to pay that back.

Relocation Expenses:

Relocation expenses cover the cost of moving and travel during the move. There are limits to what you can spend the money on and you will probably have to do a lot of paperwork to get paid. Still, this is a great benefit if you are moving for a job.

Other Things you can ask for: Flexible Schedule

With a flexible schedule, you can come in late and leave later, or come in early and leave early as long as you keep your manager and teammates in the loop. This kind of schedule may or may not be allowed at your new employer. If it is allowed it is something you will want to talk about now before you start. You have the most leverage before you show up on the first day of work.

Work from home days

Some teams allow team members to work a day or two from home. Working from home can mean less time commuting and more time with friends and family. If this sounds attractive to you, one way to bring it up politely without sounding presumptuous is after you receive your offer letter, ask. "Does anyone on the team work a day or two from home every week?" If the hiring manager says yes, then chances are pretty good you can too and you can continue the conversation. If the answer is a solid no, then this is a sign you should probably find something else to ask for.

Extra Days off

It is worth putting this on the list. If you work for a smaller employer they may be able to make this happen. Most large companies cannot grant extra days off as part of salary negotiation. If you get paid the same amount and work fewer days by definition you are making more for the work you do. Days off are precious and the more you can have the better.

Starting Earlier / Starting Later

Depending on your situation it may be more beneficial for you to start earlier so you can start collecting a paycheck. Or you may need to delay your start a few weeks. This is the time to have the discussion and find out what works for both you and your new employer.

Timing is important. Once you get an offer you are in a powerful position. It is in your best interest to take your time in deciding because you may get another offer from a different employer. Having more than one offer is the best place to be in a negotiation. Don't be pressured to take the job offer without first reading the written offer letter and taking at least 24 hours to consider the offer carefully.

There are no magic scripts in negotiation. It's important to listen to the person you are negotiating with. Often they will consciously or subconsciously tip their hand at areas where they are willing to give a little. If you aren't negotiating with the owner of the company or the CEO then the negotiator probably has some rules and parameters they do have to follow. Never get hostile. Hostility will get you nowhere and may end your chances of working there. Nobody wants to work with a jerk. It is ok to be direct if you have other options. For instance, "I have another offer from company X for XX,XXX but I'd rather work on your team, but to do so I need to make more than $XX,XXX."

Leverage is important and you will have more leverage when negotiating for your second job a few years from now. I wouldn't recommend a hardball negotiation for your first software job, but I would recommend you do some negotiation to see if you can inch up the offer a little bit. Honesty is important on both sides of the table. If you are dealing with any reputable employer you can expect to be treated honestly. Likewise, the employer deserves your honesty as well. If you do decide to accept your offer and you let them know. At that point, they will start spending money to get ready for you. They will probably create the work order to buy you a computer, set up your cubicle and start doing other things that cost money. So if you take an offer I urge you to stand by your word follow through.

Chapter 9 Action Guide

1. Make an honest attempt to negotiate salary but also realize your leverage is limited.
2. Stay positive and upbeat through the whole process.

Congratulations

Congratulations if you work hard and follow the steps in this book you put yourself at a great advantage. This chapter will help you with those critical first steps, during your first few days as the newest member of the team.

Your First 100 Days Are Key

You never get a second chance to make a first impression. You will be meeting a lot of new people and making a lot of first impressions. Chances are some of your future positions that are going to come from the relationships you establish in this first position. It's important that you seize these opening months of your career and fully use them to your advantage. Here are a few secrets I've learned along the way.

Secret 1. Dumb questions are expected for your first 30 days. Use your temporary immunity to ask lots and lots of questions. If something doesn't make sense ask more follow up questions. This is your chance to get a firm understanding of the company you work for. Ask about everything. Ask about the business and how the company manages to make a profit. Ask about career growth. Ask about the technology you work on. Ask about business processes that don't appear to make sense. Ask within the spirit of learning and it will pay dividends.

Secret 2. Your teammates do want you to succeed
Many young professionals come into the professional world thinking it's going to be like you are a contestant on Trump's

apprentice. This simply isn't the case. Most of your coworkers are going to want you to be as successful as humanly possible. Now you may meet a few trolls on your career path.

You'll find that trolls are just temporary distractions. Value comes from helping people out. People who do not provide value end up stuck in their careers and cannot move forward. Your coworkers want you to be successful because they want to be successful. Likewise, do what you can to help everyone else be successful. This brings me to secret number 3. Secret 3. Your value will be measured by the number of people you help.

Do the small things that show you care. Stay 5 minutes after the meeting to help the person who coordinated it clean up. Offer up agenda items to meetings that you participate in. Each day find a way you can help make a teammates life just 1% easier and do it. Even if it is a pain. Go out of your way to help people.

Find A Mentor

Everyone should look for a great mentor. The people who's careers grow fastest are cognizant of that fact and pick the best to emulate. The best people tend to rise to the top. It feels like this takes forever, however it's only a couple of years. When looking for a good mentor I would look for a few kinds of people. First, find one person who is currently operating at a level of competency you want to be in two years. Someone just one career stage above you who can help you learn the tactical ropes and get you up and running on the key technologies fast. You want someone who just went through what you are going through right now so that you can benefit from all of the details they have and get up to speed and producing valuable work as quickly as possible. Pick someone who others count on, someone whose skills you admire.

This relationship doesn't have to be a formal one, but there are some benefits to making it a little more formal.

Depending on your company culture you may want to ask this person to be your formal technical mentor. I'd suggest you approach the conversation something like this.
"Hi <MentorTarget>, I've been watching how you work. I appreciate your ability to <Professional Skill>. This is my first engineering job, and with so much to learn, I can use some help focusing on the right skills to develop. Will you mentor me?"

The other kind of mentor I suggest you find is someone older and happy. So many developers burn out as they get older. But others find a way to make it a joyous profession even into their 50s and 60s. You'll find that these men and women are full of wisdom and humility. Use a similar script like the one above and ask them to mentor you. This will probably be a completely different kind of mentorship compared to your other technical mentorship. The wisdom older developers have is about being a life long learner. Parts of problem solving that endure over multiple paradigms and tool sets. Even deep understanding of company operational models and the origins of certain organizational issues.

Both kinds of mentors give you an unfair advantage. Both kinds of relationships are worth investing in. A good mentor can distill 5 years of painful learning into a few conversations and save you the trouble of a stalled career.

Have the courage and humility to seek these kinds of people out. It's one of the best things I've done in my career.

Keep Learning

More are invented every day than you can learn. Keep learning anyway. The value you can create is directly related to the skills, patterns, and toolsets you learn. Make learning new things a professional priority. Find ways to learn and teach your teammates. Practice what you learn to make it stick. Teach what you learn on your blog, a podcast, or youtube.

The best developers learn faster than mediocre ones. And the value of learning is exponential. Skills, tools, and paradigms gather exponential value. When you stop learning, you will start the timer until the end of your career. Technology changes too fast, your skills will expire. What you know will become irrelevant. What you learn will dictate how much you can earn. There are several great ways to keep learning.

Side Projects:

Side projects give you the freedom to experiment, build and fail on your own. They are a chance to learn without limits and try things that are against the rules within your company's VPN. They are a great way to try new tools and techniques.

Online Courses:

Online courses like Team Treehouse, Pluralsight or Coursera are great for quickly learning the basics of new concepts and technologies. Many employers will pay for the courseware if it's being used. These are a great way to help stay current.

Developer Meetups:

Developer meetups and hackathons are a great place to work with new people and learn new techniques. It's a good place to see how others work and take the best of their practices and include them in your daily routines.

Wrapping up:

It doesn't matter how you decide to learn. What matters is that you continually learn new things and stay current. If you don't the world will quickly move out from underneath you. This is just the beginning. You have a very bright future ahead.